HOW TURTLES GROW UP

Linda Bozzo

E **Enslow Publishing**
101 W. 23rd Street
Suite 240
New York, NY 10011
USA
enslow.com

WORDS TO KNOW

clutch A group of eggs laid about the same time.

flippers Two flat body parts that stick out from the side of some turtles and are used for swimming.

hatchlings Baby turtles.

insects Small animals with six legs and a body with three parts that may also have wings.

predators Animals that kill and eat other animals to live.

reptiles Animals that have cold blood, lay eggs, and have a body covered with scales or hard parts like a shell.

species A group of the same kind of living thing that have the same scientific name.

webbed feet Feet with pieces of skin between the toes.

CONTENTS

REPTILES

Turtles are reptiles. They move very slowly. They have hard shells to protect themselves. Turtles can be found nearly all over the world.

FAST FACT

Turtles are among the oldest members of the reptile family.

Turtles have been around since the age of the dinosaurs!

LAYING EGGS

All turtles lay eggs. Some species lay just a few eggs. Other species may lay 100 eggs or more! A group of eggs in a turtle nest is called a clutch.

A clutch of turtle eggs lie on a beach.

FAST FACT

Sea turtles return to the same place where they were born to lay their eggs.

BUILDING NESTS

Mother turtles make nests. They bury their eggs in soil, in sand, or among plants. This helps keep the eggs warm. Hiding her eggs also keeps them safe.

FAST FACT

Most mother turtles leave their nests and the eggs on their own.

A mother turtle buries her eggs in the sand.

9

EGGS HATCH

When the eggs hatch depends on the species. Most babies will start to break out of their eggs after about two months. Baby turtles are called hatchlings.

Hatchlings have an egg tooth they use to break out of their shells.

A tortoise hatchling breaks out of its egg.

11

MALE OR FEMALE?

For many species, the temperature in the nest decides the sex of the hatchlings. Warmer nests mean more females. Cooler nests mean more males.

FAST FACT

Turtles grow very slowly during their lifetime.

A turtle hatchling is on its own as soon as it is born.

RESTING FOR A WHILE

Hatchlings stay in the nest for a few days to rest. They build up their strength. Then they climb out of their nest. Many head straight to the water.

Sea turtles can sleep underwater.

Baby sea turtles make their way to the ocean.

MANY DANGERS

Once out of their nest, the hatchlings face many dangers. Hungry raccoons, birds, and fish are just a few of the predators they might face.

Some mother turtles guard their eggs for a while. But they don't take care of their young.

A vulture grabs a baby sea turtle. Many turtle hatchlings are eaten by predators before they reach the water.

17

WHAT'S FOR DINNER?

Different species eat different kinds of food. Some turtles eat plants such as grasses, fruit, and flowers. Others eat small animals such as fish, worms, and insects. Some eat both plants and meat.

A baby tortoise munches on a leaf. Most tortoises eat only plants.

FAST FACT

Turtles do not have teeth. A turtle uses the hard, sharp edges of its mouth to bite.

WATER AND LAND

Some hatchlings have webbed feet or flippers for swimming. They live mostly in water. Some hatchlings have claws for digging. They live mostly on land. Tortoises are turtles that live only on land.

A tortoise's shell is more dome-shaped than a turtle's. Tortoise feet are rounder and flatter, too.

SUN TIME

Freshwater turtles live in ponds and lakes. Sea turtles live in the ocean. Baby turtles often sit on rocks or logs. They like to warm themselves in the sun.

A baby turtle suns itself on a log.

FAST FACT

It is thought that sea turtles can live up to 50 years or more!

LEARN MORE

Books

Borgert-Spaniol, Megan. *Baby Turtles*. Minneapolis, MN: Bellwether Media, 2016.

Brannon, Cecelia. *Baby Turtles at the Zoo*. New York, NY: Enslow Publishing, 2016.

Duhaime, Darla. *Turtles*. Vero Beach, FL: Rourke Educational Media, 2017.

Websites

National Geographic Kids: Green Sea Turtles
kids.nationalgeographic.com/animals/green-sea-turtle/
Read about the world's largest species of hard-shelled sea turtle.

San Diego Zoo Kids: Shell Show-and-Tell
kids.sandiegozoo.org/index.php/stories/shell-show-and-tell
Learn how to tell the difference between turtles and tortoises.

INDEX

Published in 2020 by Enslow Publishing, LLC.
101 W. 23rd Street, Suite 240, New York, NY 10011

Copyright © 2020 by Enslow Publishing, LLC.

Library of Congress Cataloging-in-Publication Data

Names: Bozzo, Linda, author.
Title: How turtles grow up / Linda Bozzo.
Description: New York : Enslow Publishing, 2020. | Series: Animals growing up | Audience: K to Grade 3. | Includes bibliographical references and index.
Identifiers: LCCN 2018046990| ISBN 9781978507234 (library bound) | ISBN 9781978508316 (paperback) | ISBN 9781978508323 (6 pack)
Subjects: LCSH: Turtles—Development—Juvenile literature. | Turtles—Infancy—Juvenile literature.
Classification: LCC QL666.C5 B69 2020 | DDC 597.92—dc23
LC record available at https://lccn.loc.gov/2018046990

Printed in the United States of America

Photo Credits: Cover, p. 1 Elena Kouptsova -Vasic/Shutterstock.com; interior pages 4–23 (background), 15 (main photo) Susan M Jackson/Shutterstock.com; p. 5 J.Rangubphai/Shutterstock.com; p. 7 © iStockphoto.com/antpkr; p. 9 © iStockphoto.com/Goad1; pp. 11, 21 seasoning_17/Shutterstock.com; p. 13 elegeyda/Shutterstock.com; p. 17 Yuri Cortez/AFP/Getty Images; p. 19 Brandon Rosenblum/Moment Open/Getty Images; p. 21 Lawrence Billiter/Shutterstock.com; back cover and additional interior pages background graphic 13Imagery/Shutterstock.com.